POWER of PATTERNS

FRACTALS

Theo Buchanan

Consultants

Timothy Rasinski, Ph.D.
Kent State University

Lori Oczkus, M.A.
Literacy Consultant

Publishing Credits

Rachelle Cracchiolo, M.S.Ed., *Publisher*
Conni Medina, M.A.Ed., *Managing Editor*
Dona Herweck Rice, *Series Developer*
Emily R. Smith, M.A.Ed., *Content Director*
Stephanie Bernard/Noelle Cristea, M.A.Ed., *Editors*
Robin Erickson, *Senior Graphic Designer*

The TIME logo is a registered trademark of TIME Inc. Used under license.

Image Credits: Cover page (front) Laguna Design/Science Source, (back) James Oakley/Alamy Stock Photo; pp. 6-7 Don Johnston_ON/Alamy Stock Photo; pp. 10–11 Alamy_AWK44H_hires. jpg; ap.16 Jesse Kraft/Alamy Stock Photo; p.17 (top) R. Williams (STScI), the Hubble Deep Field Team and NASA/ESA, (middle) NASA, ESA, H. Teplitz and M. Rafelski (IPAC/Caltech), A. Koekemoer (STScI), R. Windhorst (Arizona State University), and Z. Levay (STScI), (bottom) NASA; ESA; G. Illingworth, D. Magee, and P. Oesch, University of California, Santa Cruz; R. Bouwens, Leiden University; and the HUDF09 Team; p.19 (top and middle) Custom Life Science Images/Alamy Stock Photo, (bottom) PAUL D STEWART/SCIENCE PHOTO LIBRARY; p.21 Antiqua Print Gallery/Alamy Stock Photo; p.25 Alexander Vasenin/Wikimedia Commons License: Creative Commons BY-SA 3.0/https://goo.gl/hEO3zZ; p.26 The Science Picture Company/Phototake; p.27 SPL/Science Source; p.28 allOver images/Alamy Stock Photo; p.29 Kage Mikrofotografie/Phototake; p.33 (top) Debivort/Wikimedia Commons License: Creative Commons BY-SA 3.0/https://goo.gl/x05j1H, (bottom) Ted Kinsman/Science Source; p.34 Ted Kinsman/Science Source; pp.34–35 A. T. Willett/Alamy Stock Photo; pp.36–37 Wolfgang Beyer with the program Ultra Fractal 3/Wikimedia Commons License: Creative Commons BY-SA 3.0/https://goo.gl/u8Pj9j; p.37 Science Photo Library/Alamy Stock Photo; p.41 António Miguel de Campos/Public Domain; p.42 Rutgers University Press; p.43 From the American Geographical Society Library, University of Wisconsin-Milwaukee Libraries; p.48 James Oakley/Alamy Stock Photo; back cover PAUL D STEWART/SCIENCE PHOTO LIBRARY; all other images from iStock and/or Shutterstock

Library of Congress Cataloging-in-Publication Data

Names: Buchanan, Theodore.
Title: Fractals / Theo Buchanan.
Description: Huntington Beach, CA : Teacher Created Materials, Inc., [2017] | Series: Power of patterns | Audience: Grade 7 to 8. | Includes index.
Identifiers: LCCN 2016047695 (print) | LCCN 2016048548 (ebook) | ISBN 9781493836260 (pbk.) | ISBN 9781480757301 (eBook)
Subjects: LCSH: Fractals--Juvenile literature. | Geometry--Juvenile literature. | Shapes--Juvenile literature.
Classification: LCC QA614.86 .B83 2017 (print) | LCC QA614.86 (ebook) | DDC 514/.742--dc23
LC record available at https://lccn.loc.gov/2016047695

Teacher Created Materials

5301 Oceanus Drive
Huntington Beach, CA 92649-1030
http://www.tcmpub.com
ISBN 978-1-4938-3626-0
© 2017 Teacher Created Materials, Inc.

Table of Contents

Euclid, the Tip of the Iceberg

Euclid was a Greek mathematician who wrote extensively about points, lines, and shapes. He is often referred to as the "father of geometry." For millennia, we have built on his work, creating what we use today: **Euclidean geometry**.

From where you are, how many rectangles can you spot? Circles? What about triangles? Maybe some things don't fit into these categories at all. Some shapes look very complex, but they are actually just combinations of basic ones. For example, the shape of the front of a microwave would typically be considered rectangular. But because its corners are usually rounded, it is a combination of rectangles and circles.

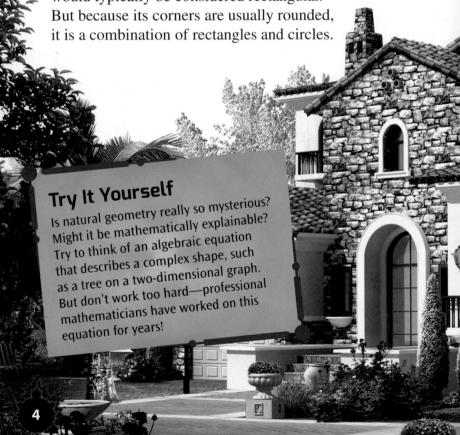

Try It Yourself

Is natural geometry really so mysterious? Might it be mathematically explainable? Try to think of an algebraic equation that describes a complex shape, such as a tree on a two-dimensional graph. But don't work too hard—professional mathematicians have worked on this equation for years!

What about Nature's Geometry?

Nature is mysterious. With the seasonal changes in scenery come changes in geometry that often seem unexplainable. But have no fear; this book will attempt to explain the unexplainable. It will show you something separate from Euclidean geometry: the geometry of fractals!

Non-Euclidean Geometry

Elliptic geometry describes geometry drawn on the surface of a sphere (such as a globe or a basketball) rather than a flat plane. Many of the basic rules of Euclidean geometry fall apart in elliptic geometry. For example, you know that the angles in a triangle always total 180 degrees. However, the angles of a triangle drawn on the surface of a sphere always total greater than 180 degrees!

The geometry of this house is rectangular, triangular, and even circular.

Introduction to Fractals

Looking at this photo of a tree, you can probably imagine roots extending into the soil below what is pictured. But what if I told you that this isn't really a tree because it's just a branch someone stuck into the snow? Isn't it easy to see how it could be both? That is because the structure of a branch is similar to that of a tree.

Branches make up trees, but they also look like smaller versions of trees. We call this **self-similarity**. In a self-similar pattern, pieces of the pattern are miniature replicas of the whole. And that means that within those replicas, there will be even smaller replicas. This replication either stops at a certain scale or continues *ad infinitum* (to infinity). Take a look at a small tree branch coming out from a larger branch and notice, again, the tree-like structure. In a large tree, you can see dozens, sometimes even hundreds of mini trees! This is an example of a fractal.

What's the Definition?

Fractals come in a huge variety of forms, but they are generally defined as shapes that exhibit self-similarity and high complexity. As you will see, these shapes appear in many different forms throughout nature.

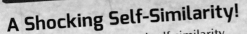

A Shocking Self-Similarity!

An example of non-fractal self-similarity hides right in plain sight: the line. It's a basic building block of Euclidean geometry. And yet, no matter how you slice it and dice it, its pieces stay the same shape as the whole. So self-similar doesn't necessarily mean fractal.

A Branching Challenge

A tree trunk grows eight feet tall and then splits into three branches. Those three branches create the second level. Each of the second-level branches grows four feet before splitting into three more branches of two feet each, which make up the third level. For each level that follows the third level, each branch splits into three more branches. If the tree continues to grow with each new branch half the length of the one it grew from, how long is the branching path from the bottom of the tree to the tip of a fifth-level branch? And how many fifth-level branches are there?

Fractals Everywhere!

"Why is geometry often described as 'cold' and 'dry'? One reason lies in its inability to describe the shape of a cloud, a mountain, a coastline, or a tree. Clouds are not spheres, mountains are not cones, coastlines are not circles."

—*Mathematician and "fractalist" Benoit Mandelbrot*

Very Few People Know . . .

Even gently sloping and hilly terrain is often fractal—mounds made of smaller mounds made of smaller mounds. Though not always dramatic or easily noticeable, fractals are in the natural landscapes all around us.

Fractal geometry is a mathematical infant. The term *fractal* has only existed since Mandelbrot, the "father of fractals," published his book, *The Fractal Geometry of Nature*, in 1982. This is amazing because for as long as humans have inhabited Earth, they have been surrounded by these patterns, and not in any small way either. As Mandelbrot points out, some of the largest features of our planet are fractals.

In comics, mountains are often shown as triangles. Even a photograph of a mountain will often appear to be roughly triangular, but this triangle is rough because it is made up of many smaller triangles. These smaller triangles are rough because they are also made up of smaller ones, and so on.

A Mountainous Comparison

The longest mountain range in the world is the Andes, which stretches along the whole west coast of South America, a total of approximately 4,500 miles. In terms of area, it takes up 1.3 million square miles. The Rocky Mountain range of western North America is 3,000 miles long and 382,894 square miles. What is the ratio of the average width of the Andes to the average width of the Rockies?

The Coastline Paradox

On an atlas, you won't find any perfectly smooth continents. In fact, not only are Earth's landmasses complex and jagged, but they also show even more complexity as you zoom in. *Roughness* is an important aspect of fractal geometry because it is a big departure from Euclidean geometry, in which shapes are smooth.

How do we measure something jagged like a coastline when we can only use lines? Well, when measuring non-straight lengths, connecting short lines yields an accurate measurement. It's always possible to use even shorter lines to measure, and in doing so, the length becomes longer and longer, approaching **infinity**! The areas of landmasses are finite because they are constrained by coastlines. They don't go on forever. So then, how can the coastlines, the boundaries between land and water, be infinite? This is called the Coastline **Paradox**. It demonstrates how difficult it is to describe nature with Euclidean geometry.

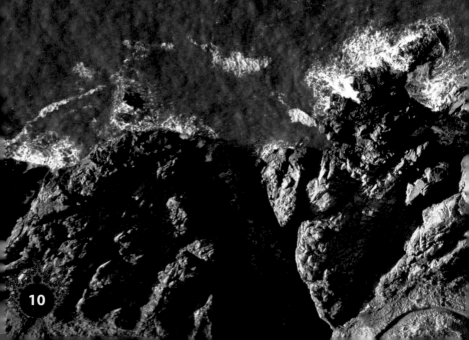

- Do you think it's possible to determine the fully accurate measurement of anything? Why or why not?
- What are some features that make geometric figures more complex to measure?

Measurements

It seems clear that complex natural things are impossible to measure accurately. Now, consider something made by people, such as a rectangular suitcase. In theory, it would be easy to measure the dimensions of a suitcase with no pockets or rounded corners. But in reality, suitcases have marks, dents on the edges, and tiny rips in the stitching. That makes measuring them accurately much more difficult.

Another way of describing self-similarity is *scale invariance*. Scale invariance means that there is no change, or variance, in pattern between the large scale and the small. Zooming in on a particular part of a scale-invariant pattern will yield the same image as seen when observing the pattern in its entirety. Determining a variance is difficult because there is no change in structure between the small scale and the large scale.

The same is true for a drawing of a mountain. It looks as though it could be massive and might take weeks to climb, or it could just be the drawing of the top of a mountain, needing only a single afternoon's climb. Therefore, mountains exhibit scale invariance.

Fluffy Fractals!

A photo taken of a cloud formation up close will also show a remarkable level of scale invariance. This is because each individual "puff" is made up of smaller puffs.

Clouds are good examples of why the term *fractal* doesn't need a strict definition. It's nearly always true that each puff has a somewhat unique shape, so clouds are really not *strictly* self-similar. But because all the shapes are so random, clouds are definitely scale invariant, making them fractals.

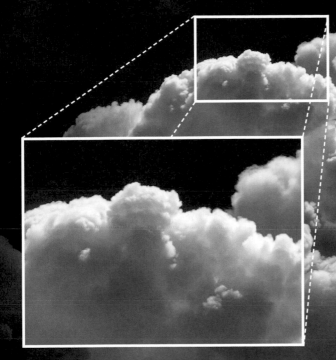

Powerful Clouds

Cumulonimbus clouds are wide, tall, and tower over other clouds. They can produce lightning, hail, and occasionally tornadoes, so airplane pilots see them as dangerous.

The Logarithmic Spiral

The logarithmic spiral is no ordinary spiral. An ordinary spiral, maintaining the same distance between each coil, is called an *Archimedean spiral*, shown below. And it's quite boring when compared to a logarithmic spiral shown to the right.

- The logarithmic spiral gets larger exponentially while it turns at a constant degree.

- This spiral can go on forever in either direction. It is a paradox because it has also been proven to have a finite length.

- The logarithmic spiral shows scale invariance. Zooming in or out, the shape will stay the same.

- Still, it is important to note that this shape is *not* considered a fractal. It shows self-similarity, yes, but centered only around the center of the shell. The nature of a fractal is to show self-similarity in many areas, which in turn show self-similarity in many areas themselves. This is what leads to extreme roughness and complexity, which the logarithmic spiral lacks.

Archimedean spiral

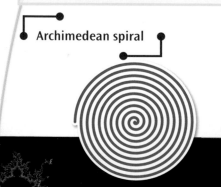

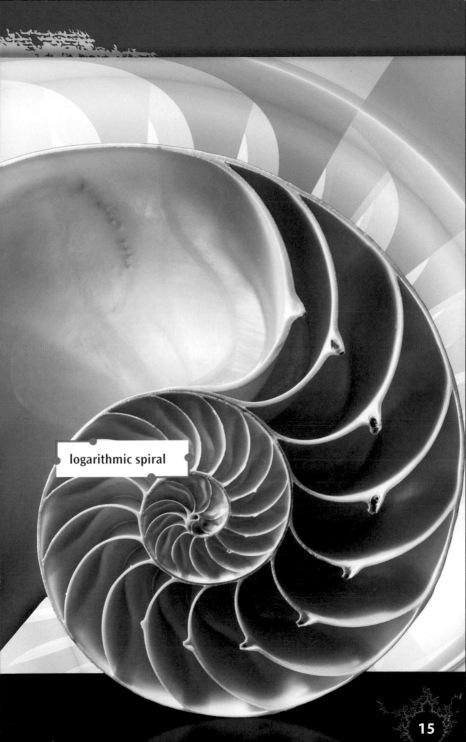

logarithmic spiral

Everyday Fractals

Not all fractals are strict geometric shapes. A **humbling** example of this is the fractal nature of our perspective of space. Fractal researcher Michael Barnsley said of the Milky Way, "It's got an extraordinary dotty character and yet, if . . . you look at it ever closer, you find . . . thousands more little dots where you thought there were almost none. [It's] a structure that seems to go in and in and in with more and more detail."

But this fractal perspective goes far beyond our little Milky Way. In 1995, astronomers pointed the Hubble Space Telescope at what seemed to be a completely empty patch of space. They kept it pointed there for 10 whole days. This was thought to be a waste of a precious scientific resource. A lot of people expected the result to be a solid black photograph.

The developed photo assembled from 342 different snapshots, however, contained a whopping 3,000 galaxies—some beautifully spiral, others appearing only as distant dots. This famous photo is called the *Hubble Deep Field.*

Ancient Galaxies!

The modern scientific consensus is that the universe is 13.7 billion years old. If that's true, the *Hubble eXtreme Deep Field* shows galaxies that came into existence shortly after the beginning of the universe. Of the galaxies depicted, some are up to 13.3 billion years old.

Hubble Deep Field

Hubble Ultra-Deep Field

Zoom, Zoom, Zoom

NASA has since assembled two additional photos using the Hubble Space Telescope. In 2004, it snapped the *Hubble Ultra-Deep Field* and in 2012 the *Hubble eXtreme Deep Field*, which was shot over 23 days.

Hubble eXtreme Deep Field

Spiral Shells

Some **cephalopods**, such as nautiluses, are known for their spiral shells (like the one on page 15). At first glance, nautiluses may seem as though their shells are fractals because they show scale invariance. However, because the nautilus shell only shows self-similarity if zoomed in on the center, it cannot qualify as a fractal.

While it may be tempting to exclude all shells from being fractals, there was a lesser-known cephalopod that was fractal. Ancient **ammonites**, relatives of nautiluses, had logarithmic spiral shells. But why are ammonite shells fractal and the nautiluses' aren't?

Ammonite shells, shown on page 19, were comprised of gas chambers. The chambers fit together along seams, or **sutures**, which are often highly complex and fractal. Can you see it? Maybe the lines just appear wiggly, but can you see that the wiggles themselves wiggle? And many of those wiggles wiggle as well.

Why are fractals present in the shells of this ancient mollusk? No one seems to know for sure. The prevailing assumption is that a simple linear suture is too easily broken. An interlocking jigsaw-type pattern is stronger and more adept at handling the pressure of deep ocean environments. Whatever the reason, evolution had its way, and ammonite sutures became more and more fractal—that is, until the ammonites' extinction.

Cranial Sutures

Sutures, the seamlike areas between two bones, are also present in the skulls of mammals, only sealing fully when the brain is full-sized. The skull sutures, or cranial sutures, of deer are standout fractals.

Ammonites by Any Other Name

Ancient Greeks and Romans believed ammonite fossils could affect dreams, even causing **prophetic** dreaming. British people knew them as snakestones. The Blackfeet tribe in the United States calls them buffalo stones for their resemblance to sleeping buffaloes.

Ancients of the Plant World

Fractals are known for being incredibly complex and intricate. But there is also something very simple about them. A fractal pattern is a pattern that repeats within itself. While they are outwardly complex, the formation is basic: It's just the same function repeated at every scale. This is why fractals make so much evolutionary sense—they allow the shape and size of a plant or animal to expand on a scale with ease and logic.

A great example of this is the fern. Ferns are an ancient family of plants; they emerged some 360 million years ago. Far older than any land animals known today and older still than the dinosaurs, ferns blanketed Earth for 200 million years before the evolution of flowering plants. Now, most ferns grow under forest **canopies**, but for millions of years, they were the trees themselves.

A Frond's Fractal Form

When a leaf is made up of many smaller leaves, it is said to be *pinnate*, and the smaller leaves are called *pinnae*. Fern **fronds** often show the remarkable property of being bipinnate, which means the pinnae are made of even smaller **pinnules**. And a pinnulet is a third division of a pinnate leaf! A fractal enthusiast's favorite fern is, of course, tripinnate.

Don't Be Such a Fiddlehead!

Fern fronds are the leaves of a fern plant. They start as tightly curled spirals called *fiddleheads*. These spirals are logarithmic. Of course, what's truly amazing is that these fiddleheads also roll out, or unfurl. Think of it this way: *Fern fronds unfurl fractally from fiddleheads.*

A Pinnate Problem

A fern frond is made of 24 pinnae, which are each made of 18 pinnules, and those are each made of 12 pinnulets. What is the ratio of the total number of pinnulets to the total number of pinnae?

pinnate

bipinnate

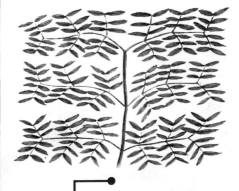

tripinnate

Romanesco Broccoli

Broccoli and geometry? Some people might think it would be hard to find two things less interesting. Romanesco broccoli proves them wrong! The striking self-similarity and complexity of this vegetable jumps right out, making it an obvious fractal. As for the actual arrangement of the "cones," they form rows that spiral logarithmically all the way down! And of course, they do so at every level of the fractal. Even more incredibly, spirals run both clockwise and counterclockwise, forming the double spiral patterns. This type of spiral can also be seen in the seeds of sunflowers.

Boring Old Broccoli?

The Fibonacci sequence is a famous number sequence that follows a simple rule: each successive number is equal to the sum of the previous two. But what does this have to do with broccoli? The Fibonacci sequence is embedded in the growth patterns of Romanesco broccoli. The number of spirals in each direction are often consecutive Fibonacci numbers.

1, 1, 2, 3, 5, 8, 13, 21, 34, 55, 89, 144 . .

Double, Double

Phyllotaxis is the technical term for an arrangement pattern of leaves or seeds. The double spiral is a common phyllotaxis pattern. It can be found in pinecones, pineapples, sunflower seeds, and even on the feathered tails of peacocks! It is the result of subtle mathematical relationships involving the **golden ratio**, the determining ratio of the Fibonacci sequence.

What on Earth?

There may be fractal aspects within the anatomy of many species. The shell of a **crustacean** might be fractal, but not the rest of it. At first glance, it could appear that the animal kingdom has no fully fractal animals to offer. Try to think of an animal with a completely fractal structure. Having trouble? Well, you're not alone. No one could, until researchers discovered a remarkable creature in 2010 that lives 1,800 feet (549 meters) below sea level in the Mid-Atlantic Ridge.

This strange-looking creature is called the *basket star*, a relative of the simple and familiar starfish. Instead of a five-point star shape, its arms branch in every direction in an incredibly fractal manner. Also known as the Gorgon head starfish, this unique animal spends all day coiled up in a ball. At night, it spreads its full fan of arms and faces the current, catching and eating plankton and shrimp. This creature shows more self-similarity than any other known animal on Earth.

Ancient Ferns

Rangeomorphs were fractal fern-like plants that existed 565 million years ago. These beautiful fractal forms are so peculiar that scientists were originally unsure whether they were plants, animals, or part of another kingdom of life altogether!

basket star

Beautiful or Frightening?

While basket stars are strangely beautiful, they do seem a bit like horror movie monsters. After all, they lie in wait all day, rising at night to pull in helpless prey with their tentacles. They even have sharp hooks growing all over each arm.

Fractals in Us

It took a search at 1,800 feet (549 meters) below sea level for researchers to encounter a wholly fractal animal. But what about the parts you can't see? What about the fractals that are inside animals? Look no further than your own body!

Scientists had long debated the composition of the brain. In 1888, Santiago Ramón y Cajal showed that the human brain is actually made from tons of individual cells called **neurons**. He found that ever-changing structures of branches called **dendrites** are attached to these neurons. Dendrites detect electricity from other neurons, and this electricity flashes around the brain in complex webs. Ramón y Cajal used a metaphor to explain that the brain is constantly changing and adapting. He compared the brain to "a garden filled with innumerable trees."

A Popular Fractal

Dendritic describes various types of branching patterns. The word *dendrite* actually stems from the Greek word *dendron*, which means *tree*. Dendritic patterns are the most common form of fractal. Aside from the dendrites in the brain, there are two more dendritic patterns in the body—the movements of blood in the body and of oxygen into the lungs.

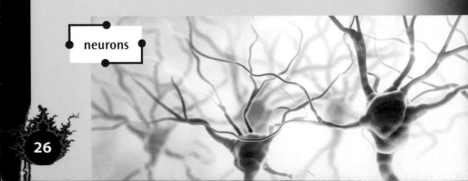

neurons

26

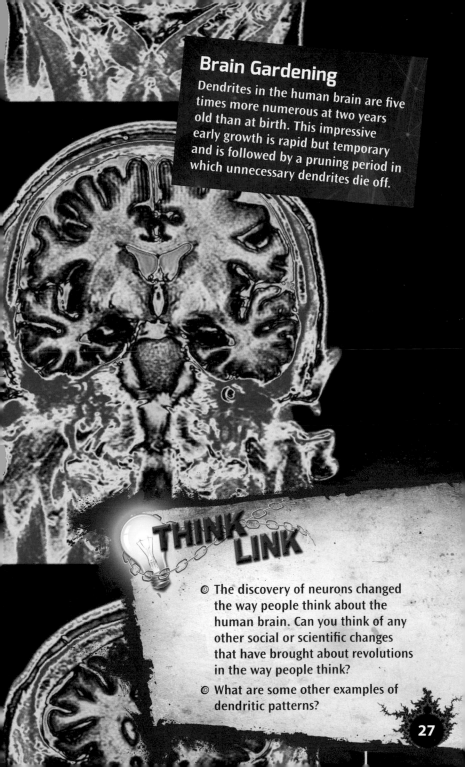

Brain Gardening

Dendrites in the human brain are five times more numerous at two years old than at birth. This impressive early growth is rapid but temporary and is followed by a pruning period in which unnecessary dendrites die off.

THINK LINK

◎ The discovery of neurons changed the way people think about the human brain. Can you think of any other social or scientific changes that have brought about revolutions in the way people think?

◎ What are some other examples of dendritic patterns?

The Venous System

Arteries and veins form a network called the **venous system**. It has a highly complex dendritic structure, with branches like those of a tree. The system is also a great example of how useful dendritic fractals can be. Organs and muscles constantly require oxygen-rich blood and other nutrients for power. The venous system's job is to keep blood in constant supply for not only the major body parts, but for every little nook and cranny. A dendritic blood-flow pattern makes a great delivery system. This is because veins can divide as much as necessary to fill small spaces such as fingers and toes. The venous system of any one part of the body is structured similarly to that of the whole body. That's what makes it a fractal.

Incredible Distance!

If you were to lay out all the blood vessels in an average child in one long line, they would stretch more than 60,000 miles. The **circumference** of Earth at the equator is 24,874 miles. Hypothetically, how many times would the blood vessels of the average child wrap around the world?

When we breathe in oxygen, how does it enter the venous system? Well, it has to pass through another fractal. The windpipe is way too thick to allow oxygen to **transfuse** into the blood, so it branches into a dendritic system called the bronchial tubes. These tubes eventually become so thin they can transmit oxygen directly into the blood. To get to this ideal size from the wide windpipe, they must divide into over 300 million *alveoli*, which exchange oxygen and carbon dioxide when people breathe in and out.

Not Quite Equal

In human lungs, the left lung is slightly smaller than the right lung because it contains a cardiac notch, in which the heart is nestled.

This human lung shows the alveoli in yellow, arteries in blue, and veins in red.

More Dendritic Fractals

Trees might be the most obvious dendritic fractals. Yet people pass them every day without realizing this. They're so massive that it's even easy to forget they're plants! Due to their ages and sizes, trees are the dinosaurs of the plant kingdom—and they haven't gone extinct! So if the fact that trees literally provide the oxygen you breath doesn't intrigue you enough, try thinking of them as *fractal plant dinosaurs of the modern era*!

Trees have been used to symbolize divinity, power, and immortality all around the world. Not only that, there is an incredible variety of species. Understanding their fractal nature goes a long way in the appreciation of tree life. In particular, it is striking how characteristics of trunk shape often apply to other levels of the tree as the trunk branches into smaller segments. Take the baobab tree for example. It is incredibly stocky and proportionally short. This can be seen in all of its branching segments. The bristlecone pine has very distinct twisted wood that is extraordinary to see once it has grown into a fractal as well.

The Tree of Life

The Tree of Life is a symbol in Norse mythology. An organization called OneZoom is building a digital Tree of Life index for all the species on Earth. The tree uses a fractal model to leave **infinite** space for new discoveries.

A Historic Pine

One of the oldest trees in the world, a bristlecone pine tree in eastern California, started growing in 3048 BC. How old is it?

Leaves: Beautiful *and* Fractal

In examining the fractal nature of a tree, it's important not to ignore the leaves, since they are direct continuations of dendritic patterns. On a rotting leaf, when the veins are all that are left, they are sometimes called skeletons. This is because the leaves' vein systems provide them with structural support—just like skeletons.

Canopy Craziness

This continuation of the dendritic pattern makes trees more fractal than ever. But what's crazier is that the shape of the canopy is fractal in a completely different way. This new fractal pattern is actually most apparent on heads of cauliflower, which look like miniature trees. The cauliflower florets people eat are usually pieces that have been broken off a larger head, but it can be hard to tell since each piece looks like a smaller version of the whole head. This is also true looking from above at its "canopy." The canopy is made of bumps, which are made of smaller bumps, and so on.

Venation Patterns in Leaves

arcuate
secondary veins
bending toward apex

cross-venulate
small veins connecting
secondary veins

dichotomus
veins branching
symmetrically in pairs

longitudinal
veins aligned mostly
along axis of leaf

palmate
several primary veins
diverging from a point

parallel
veins branching
symmetrically in pairs

pinnate
secondary veins paired
oppositely

reticulate
smaller veins forming
a network

rotate
in peltate leaves,
veins radiating

STOP! THINK...

Leaves show many different types of vein structures, or *venation*. The chart above names some common forms found in different kinds of plants. But not all venation patterns have names, and new plant discoveries are made all the time. Check out the thick veins on the bottom of this giant lily pad in the picture on the right.

- Is this a venation pattern you can find on the chart? If not, what would you name it?
- Are the veins fractal? Explain your answer.

It's All Downstream from Here!

Dendritic fractals are all over the place in the plant world, but they can also be seen on much larger scales. River systems viewed from above are particularly awe-inspiring fractals. As they flow downhill, they branch into smaller streams, each of which continues to flow and branch on its own. Why do rivers do this? They are simply running through fractal terrain and obeying the laws of gravity.

Even Electricity?

Here one microsecond and gone the next, lightning is beautifully fractal but unfortunately does not stay around long enough to really see. So how does one analyze lightning's fractal structure? Photographs work pretty well, but they eliminate the three-dimensional element. Probably the best way is to discharge high-voltage electricity through a block of insulating material, which creates a 3-D fractal sculpture such as the one shown in the picture to the right. Don't try this at home, though! It can be very dangerous and tricky, and you'd need a **particle accelerator** anyway.

Another way to analyze lightning fractals is to study the scars it leaves on people who have been struck. People who survive lightning strikes are likely to have dendritic scars on their bodies.

A Shocking Statistic!

On average, lightning strikes our planet 100 times per second. Here's a challenge: How many times on average would lightning strike within 48 hours?

The Massive and Mathe-Magical Mandelbrot!

"It's not easy to describe the Mandelbrot set visually. It looks like a man. It looks like a cat. It looks like a cactus. It looks like a cockroach. It's got little bits and pieces of almost anything you can see out in the real world—particularly living things."

—Ian Stewart, mathematician

A Mandelbrot set (shown below) is a set of complex numbers that has an intricate fractal edge. This set caused jaws to drop in the field of geometry when French mathematician Benoit Mandelbrot first revealed its bottomless depths. The set's beauty and complexity can be most appreciated when viewed on a computer. That's because regardless of how far one zooms into its complexity, the same strange shape continues to emerge.

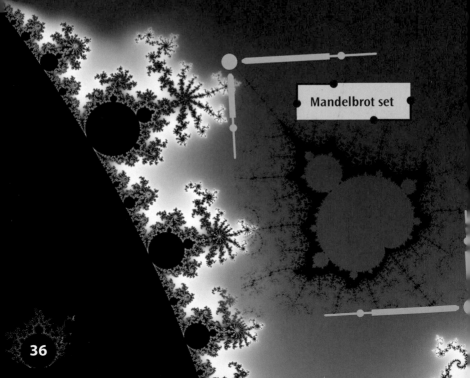

Mandelbrot set

Julia Sets

Mandelbrot discovered the set while having some "mindless fun" with Julia sets. While this might sound like a person, a Julia set is another type of fractal (shown to the right). It was discovered by Gaston Julia, a mathematician who once taught Mandelbrot. Julia sets also show up repeatedly and in many forms in the Mandelbrot set.

Fractal Imagination

Portions of the Mandelbrot set have been named based on the fractal forms that the edges take. For example, the image below is one called Seahorse Valley. Can you see the seahorses in the fractals?

The Fractal Future

Why are so many natural things fractal? The best answer comes from the *constructal law*. The constructal law says that any system of movement or growth must evolve in a way that allows following the path of least resistance. Think of how our lungs are designed to easily allow air in and out; the flow of air is smooth and unresisted.

So how do fractals do this? Remember that while a fractal looks complex, its design is very basic. A fractal is just one process repeated within itself. In achieving a given goal, such as flexibility in ferns, fractals are the path of least resistance for evolution. Simplistically speaking, fractals follow basic instructions. Remember the tongue twister from page 20? We can keep adding to it infinitely: *fern fronds unfurl fractally from fiddleheads that unfurl more fiddleheads*. A species will keep repeating these same simple instructions until it is absolutely necessary to adapt and change. It isn't scientific fact, but the constructal law gives a good explanation for the presence of fractals in nature.

Adrian Bejan

Adrian Bejan, an American professor of mechanical engineering, coined the term *constructal law*. He first formulated it in 1996 and has since written a number of articles and books on the topic.

A Universal Theory

The constructal law can be applied to everything from the veins of the human body to river systems.

a fiddlehead

Fractals are all over the place in nature, and humanity has noticed. British mathematician Michael Barnsley said, "There will be new devices, new extraordinary devices based on the principles of fractal geometry that will emerge over the next centuries."

Fractal Camo

Companies that design camouflage have started using fractal geometry to make the pattern look more natural. This method has proven to blend much better than typical camouflage patterns. In fact, the Netherlands recently made fractal camo the standard pattern for army uniforms.

Fractal Compression

Fractal compression is a rival of jpeg compression, a process that shrinks photos and images to small files. But, in doing so, jpeg compression significantly reduces the quality of images. Fractal compression, on the other hand, works by finding small parts of an image that resemble larger parts. These small parts are converted into "fractal codes." The fractal codes are then used to decode full-size images with no loss in quality. Still, fractal compression has yet to catch on. This is because coding takes a long time.

Nature as Teacher

Biomimicry is a field of design that focuses on mimicking nature. Nature has been designing itself for billions of years. So we have a lot to learn! Fractal geometry is a great example of natural design.

Landscape Forgeries

Fractals are great for designing realistic landscapes. All one must do is repeat a process over and over at smaller and smaller scales. This is called *procedural generation*. It's super efficient. Artists and designers use this process when developing movies and video games.

Why Does It Matter?

Fractal geometry reaches beyond even the realms of mathematics and science. It has been applied to topics such as philosophy, psychology, and literature—and there are surely more to come. It is even widely thought to be a key to reversing the effects of climate change! Fractal geometry is the first large break from its Euclidean counterpart. People have been stuck with a purely Euclidean understanding of the shapes that surround us for such a long time, and now it's becoming clear there are shortcomings to this. Fractal geometry has caused a **paradigm shift** that will undoubtedly have wide-ranging effects in the future.

But Mom, I'm Drawing Fractals!

Benoit Mandelbrot himself said he made his famous discovery while having "mindless fun," and **geometers** around the world have enjoyed creating their own fractals from simple sets of rules. So get curious and get creative! Fractals are out in the world to be seen and are living in your mind, waiting to be created.

New Science, Ancient Concept

Humanity has shown some signs of knowing about of fractal geometry long before coining the term "fractal" and writing mathematical **treatises** on the subject. The settlement in Zambia in the image to the right was first photographed in 1944. It is a great example of fractal geometry employed in architecture.

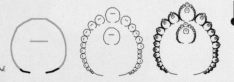

simplified breakdown showing the fractal nature of the photo to the right

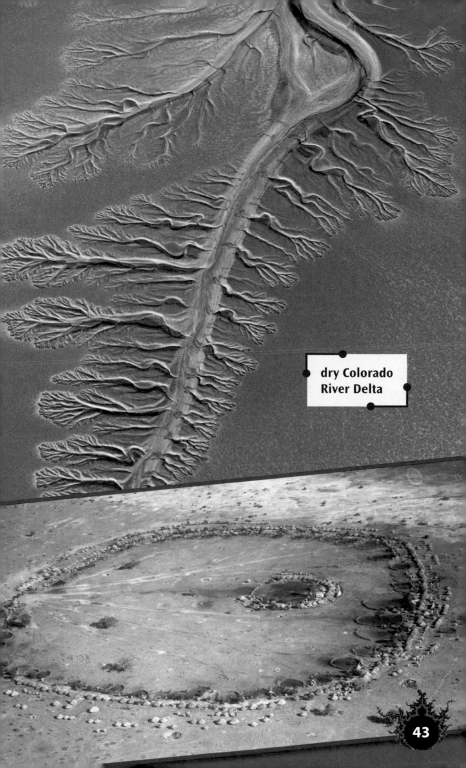

dry Colorado
River Delta

Glossary

ammonites—relatives of the nautilus that have logarithmic spiral shells but are distinguished by their fractal sutures

canopies—the topmost layers of forests or trees

cephalopods—mollusks that usually have at least eight arms and move by expelling water from tubes on their heads

circumference—the outer edge of a shape

crustacean—an animal that has many pairs of legs, a body made from sections, and an exoskeleton

dendrites—branched projections from neuron cells in the brain that pick up on electrical impulses

Euclidean geometry—geometry based on the fundamental principles of Euclid; standard geometry

fronds—leafy parts of palms, ferns, or similar plants

geometers—people who study geometry

golden ratio—a number that equals 1.618

humbling—making one feel less important

infinity—a very high number or great amount

neurons—cells that send messages from the brain to other parts of the body

paradigm shift—shift from one dominant or standard pattern of thought to another

paradox—a statement or situation about two opposite things that seem impossible but are actually possible

particle accelerator—a machine that propels charged particles to nearly light speed using electromagnetic fields

pinnules—the smaller leaves that make up the pinnae on a bipinnate plant

prophetic—predicting what will happen in the future

self-similarity—when a piece of a pattern looks like the overall pattern itself

sutures—organic seams between material

transfuse—pass from one to another

treatises—books or articles that describe a topic in great detail

venous system—the system of blood vessels in an organism

Index

Check It Out!

Books

Barnsley, Michael. 2012. *Fractals Everywhere.* Dover Publications.

Mandelbrot, Benoit B. 1982. *The Fractal Geometry of Nature.* W.H. Freeman and Company.

Mohr, Lilac. 2016. *Math and Magic in Wonderland.* CreateSpace Independent Publishing Platform.

Video

Haggit, Craig. *How Fractals Work.* http://science .howstuffworks.com/math-concepts/fractals.htm.

Websites

Fractal Foundation. http://www.fractalfoundation.org.

OneZoom. *One Zoom Tree of Life Explorer.* http://www.onezoom.org.

Try It!

Imagine your school is having a fractal art contest in a week. The award will go to the fractal design that is unique, colorful, and encompasses many different types of fractals. All designs will be scored on the following categories: *size, detail, color contrast,* and *consistency*. Before entering the contest, you have some work to do:

- Decide which types of fractals you will include in your design. Make a list of the ones you think will make for a creative piece of art. Are you going to have smooth, jagged, or straight lines? Will you have a fractal within a fractal?

- Make a list of any materials you may need. Are you creating your design digitally, on paper, or on canvas? If you are making a digital design, what program will you use? If you are making a print, do you need any drawing tools like a ruler or a protractor? Will you use pens, markers, charcoal, color pencils, or paint?

- Sketch your design.

- Color your design.

About the Author

Theo Buchanan is a writer and fractal enthusiast from Portland, Oregon, who studies philosophy at Colorado College. He is also interested in visual art, music, law, social justice, and literature.

Answers

page 7—A Branching Challenge: 15 feet 6 inches; 81 branches

page 9—A Mountainous Comparison: 2.3:1

page 21—A Pinnate Problem: 216:1

page 28—Incredible Distance!: 2.4 times

page 31—A Historic Pine: add 3,048 to current year

page 35—Shocking Statistic!: 17,280,000